SUSTAINABLE WORLD

WASTE

Rob Bowden

KIDHAVEN PRESS™

THOMSON
★
GALE

San Diego • Detroit • New York • San Francisco • Cleveland
New Haven, Conn. • Waterville, Maine • London • Munich

Commissioning Editor: Victoria Brooker
Book Designer: Jane Hawkins
Consultant: Dr. Rodney Tolley
Hodder Children's Books
A division of Hodder Headline Limited
338 Euston Road, London NW1 3BH

Book Editor: Margot Richardson
Picture Research: Shelley Noronha, Glass Onion Pictures

Cover: Forklift stacking recycled paper.

Title page: Rubbish litters this city roadside in Nigeria, creating a public waste problem.

Contents page: Waste plastic is sorted for recycling in New Delhi, India.

Picture credits: Cover: Getty Images (V.C.L.) 17, (Robert Landau) 39; EASI-Images (Rob Bowden) 7 (bottom), 16, 23 (left), 25, 45, (Roy Maconachie) 22, 23 (right), 28; Ecoscene (L A Raman) 3, (Vicki Coombs) 8, (Jim Winkley) 11, (John Wilkinson) 12, (Erik Schaffer) 15, (Alan Towse) 19, (John Farmar) 32, (Wayne Lawler) 33, (Bruce Harber) 36, (Erik Schaffer) 40, (Amanda Gazidis) 43; Getty Images (V. C. L.) cover; Impact (Peter Menzel) 30, (Piers Cavendish) 37; Peter Menzel 2003 20, 21; Popperfoto 9, (Reuters/Bobby Yip) 13, (Reuters/Henry Romero) 26, (Reuters/Toshiyuki Aizawa) 29; Still Pictures (Mark Edwards) title page, (Paul Glendell) 4, (Mark Edwards) 5, (Edgar Cleijne) 6, (Emmanuel Vialet) 7, (Hartmut Schwarzbach) 10, (Mark Edwards) 18, (Adrian Arbib) 24, (Julia Etchart) 44; Topham Picturepoint 14, (Polfoto) 27, (ANP/Bob van den Cruysem) 34, (Polfoto/Jens Dresling) 42; Hodder Wayland Picture Library 35, (Angela Hampton) 38, (Angela Hampton) 41, Wiggly Wigglers Ltd 31.

LIBRARY OF CONGRESS CATALOGING-IN-PUBLICATION DATA

Bowden, Rob
  Waste / by Rob Bowden.
    p. cm. — (Sustainable world)

Includes bibliographical references and index.

  ISBN 0-7377-1902-8 (lib. bdg. : alk. paper)

  1. Refuse and refuse disposal.
  I. Title. II. Sustainable world (Kidhaven Press)
    TD791.B65 2004

363.72–dc21   2003052951

Printed in Hong Kong

Contents

Why sustainable waste?

W E ALL PRODUCE WASTE. WHETHER AT HOME, school, work, or at leisure, all human activities create waste in one form or another. You may not give much thought to the wastes you produce in a day, but if you did you would probably be quite surprised by both the variety and amount.

WORLD OF WASTE

You are only one of almost 6.5 billion people on Earth whose activities all produce wastes. That said, not everyone produces the same amount of waste or indeed the same types of waste. In general, people living in the more developed regions of the world such as North America and Europe generate more waste than those living in less developed regions such as Asia or Africa. The fact remains, however, that at the start of the twenty-first century the amount of waste generated is growing year by year.

The endless generation of waste means landfill sites such as this in the United Kingdom are quickly becoming full.

DATABANK

An average person living in the United Kingdom throws away the equivalent of seven to ten times their own bodyweight in garbage every year.

BREAKING POINT

Coal-fired power stations release large volumes of CO_2 and other waste gases into the atmosphere.

As the volume of waste increases so does its impact on people and the environment. Some of the impact is very visible, such as litter on the streets of towns and cities, or lakes and rivers polluted by waste chemicals. Some is less visible, but extremely serious, such as the threat of climate change due to emissions of carbon dioxide (CO_2) and other greenhouse gases into the atmosphere. Around the world there are signs that something must be done to reduce the problems caused by waste and, more importantly, to reduce the amount of waste generated in the first place. Failure to act could push the Earth's ability to support life beyond breaking point. This problem has been demonstrated by the environmental group, Friends of the Earth. They believe that if everyone were to generate waste at levels similar to people living in the United Kingdom or United States today, then the equivalent of eight planets would be needed to sustain such a wasteful world in the future.

AN ALTERNATIVE FUTURE

An alternative future, one built around the idea of sustainable development, is possible. Sustainable development is about using and managing resources for the benefit of people today, while protecting and conserving them for the benefit of future generations. This book will explore the vital role waste has to play in a more sustainable world.

The waste problem

At ONE TIME, HUMAN ACTIONS PRODUCED wastes that could be absorbed by the environment. This was because they were mainly organic wastes (wastes that decompose naturally) produced from activities such as farming, hunting, and fishing. The human population was also relatively small and in 1800, around the time of the Industrial Revolution, was still less than 1 billion people.

THE PRICE OF PROGRESS

From the time of the industrial revolution, a series of scientific and technological breakthroughs have allowed humans to manipulate the natural environment for their own benefit. These breakthroughs have brought us many things that we today take for granted, including new materials such as plastics and nylon, and products such as cars, televisions and white goods (washing machines, fridges, etc). Scientific advances also allowed for dramatic improvements in people's health and life expectancy. As a result, world population grew rapidly, reaching 2 billion by 1927 and then accelerating extremely fast to reach 4 billion in 1974 and 6 billion by 1999. The world population continues to grow by around 80 million people a year and is estimated to reach 9 billion by around 2050.

Plastic goods made from oil, such as these for sale in Ghana, present new waste challenges.

DATABANK

A typical plastic bag will take around 500 years to decay in a landfill site.

Discarded plastic bags in France are caught among trees, having been blown there by the wind.

This progress comes with a price, however, often paid in the amount of waste that is produced. For example, the discovery of oil that led to the development of plastics and the dependence on cars has also led to serious waste problems such as how to manage waste plastics and the polluting emissions of motor vehicles. Progress has also led to an energy-hungry world, with most of this demand being met by fossil fuels. A problem with this is that when fossil fuels are burned (to release their energy) they emit carbon into the atmosphere which mixes with oxygen to become carbon dioxide — one of the major greenhouse gases responsible for climate change. Global carbon emissions increased from 1,637 million tons in 1950 to 6,399 million tons by 2000. This increase, of an incredible 390 percent, is much greater than the 240 percent increase in population over the same period. It shows that the amount of waste produced is increasing at a rate faster than population growth, meaning each of us is producing more waste than in the past.

Waste incineration along this roadside in Kenya causes choking, hazardous fumes.

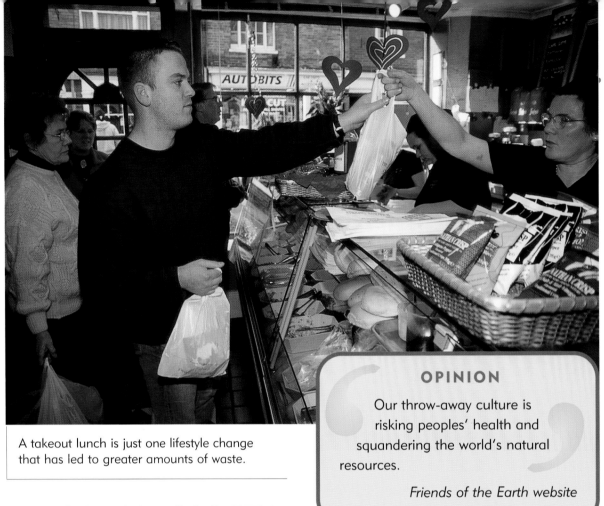

A takeout lunch is just one lifestyle change that has led to greater amounts of waste.

OPINION

Our throw-away culture is risking peoples' health and squandering the world's natural resources.

Friends of the Earth website

THROWAWAY SOCIETY

Some of the main reasons we each produce more waste than in the past is due to changing lifestyles and increased wealth. Greater wealth means people have more money to spend and are more willing (and likely) to pay for convenience in the goods they buy. This has led to an enormous increase in waste because of the packaging involved in convenience foods.

Take, for example, a typical office worker buying his or her lunch from a sandwich shop. The chances are that the sandwich is packaged (more often than not in plastic), as is a bag of chips and perhaps a couple of cookies for dessert. They may also buy a coffee in a disposable polystyrene or paper cup, or perhaps water or a soft drink in a plastic bottle, carton, or aluminium can. All of this will probably be packed in a plastic bag from the store itself and so, very quickly, this single office worker has created a significant amount of waste. Compare that to the office worker of twenty or thirty years ago who was more likely to have brought lunch from home in a reusable lunch box and a bottle or thermos. This would have produced only a minimal amount of waste, if any at all. Convenience is only one factor that has led to greater waste, however. There is also enormous pressure from advertisers to constantly try new products as fads change or to replace existing goods with new or updated ones. The cell phone market is a good example of this. In the United Kingdom, for example, people replace their cell phones, on average, every eighteen months, despite them having a useful life of around eight years. This wasteful practice results in some 15 million cell phones being replaced each year, many of which are simply thrown away. The impact of this waste is significant. For example, the cadmium from a single cell phone battery is sufficient to pollute around 160,000 gallons of water (about a third of an Olympic swimming pool). Most cell phones are simply dumped in landfill sites where such wastes can easily escape into the environment. The combination of convenience and constantly changing fads and technology, have created a consumer society that is also a throwaway society — and far from sustainable.

DATABANK

In the United Kingdom, about 1.5 million computers are thrown away every year, most of them ending up in landfills.

Cell phone companies encourage people to constantly upgrade their phones; the old ones are often just thrown away.

TYPES OF WASTE

Waste can be classified into many different types. For example, it can be described as solid, liquid, or gaseous waste, or as organic and non-organic waste. One of the most common ways to classify waste (as used by many governments) is as municipal solid waste (MSW) and industrial waste. Waste can also be classified as hazardous.

MSW is the waste that you and I have most contact with. It includes the waste from our own homes and gardens and from the schools, offices, shops, restaurants, and hospitals within our communities. It also includes the waste from public garbage cans and local trash collection sites (dumps as they are often known). When most people discuss waste it is this type of waste that they are normally talking about.

Industrial waste comes from industrial processes such as mining, energy production, manufacturing, and agriculture. Industrial waste can be produced on an enormous scale. In mining, for example, vast quantities of material are removed from the ground in order to extract the desired mineral. It is not unusual for over 75 percent of this to end up as waste, known as tailings. Other industries, such as the

Municipal solid waste (MSW) is collected from homes in Bielefeld, Germany. MSW is the waste we have most day-to-day contact with.

paper industry, produce massive quantities of waste water, much of it contaminated with chemicals from the production process.

Only a fraction of the iron ore extracted from this Australian mine is mineral that can be used.

Hazardous waste presents a danger to human health and/or the environment. As well as specific sources of hazardous waste, such wastes can also be found in MSW and industrial wastes. For example, chemicals used in certain industrial processes or the heavy metals used in batteries can both be hazardous if not properly handled. Agricultural chemicals can also be hazardous, such as some pesticides which can lead to growth disorders, blindness, or even death in both wildlife and humans. Among the most hazardous wastes are radioactive wastes. These are found in hospitals where they are used in x-ray departments, for example, and are produced in larger quantities by the nuclear energy industry. The most dangerous nuclear wastes can remain hazardous to life for a half a million years!

WASTE DISPOSAL

Just as there are different types of wastes, there are also different methods of waste disposal. The main methods include burying mixed waste in landfill sites, burning it in incinerators, and re-using or recycling sorted waste. Of these, only the re-use or recycling of waste is truly sustainable. Unfortunately though, the vast majority of waste is presently disposed of in landfills or by incineration. In the USA, for example, around 57 percent of MSW is disposed of in landfill, while in the UK this rises to 78 percent and to over 90 percent in Greece and Mexico! The incineration of MSW is a more popular disposal method in Japan, Denmark and Sweden where it accounts for 69, 54 and 42 percent of MSW disposal respectively.

Incinerators reduce solid waste to ashes, but release toxic pollutants into the atmosphere.

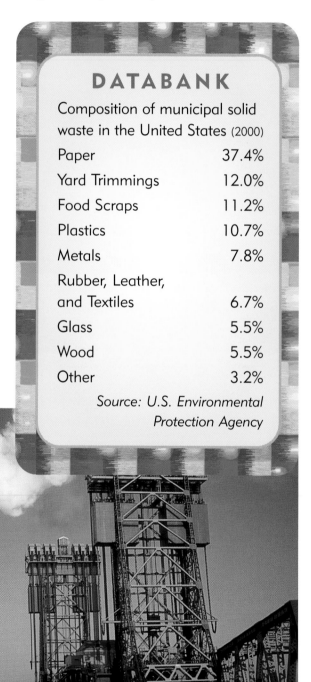

DATABANK

Composition of municipal solid waste in the United States (2000)

Paper	37.4%
Yard Trimmings	12.0%
Food Scraps	11.2%
Plastics	10.7%
Metals	7.8%
Rubber, Leather, and Textiles	6.7%
Glass	5.5%
Wood	5.5%
Other	3.2%

Source: U.S. Environmental Protection Agency

Burying waste simply buries the problems associated with waste. Many wastes will take hundreds or even thousands of years to decompose, whilst others will release toxic substances (toxins) as they break down. In some landfill sites these toxins have been absorbed by rain water to form a substance known as leachate that can then sometimes pass into the surrounding environment. In 1978, leachate that came from a landfill site in Love Canal, New York, contaminated local land and water and led to a school and housing estate being relocated.

Incineration of mixed wastes is not much better as the burning process can release toxins into the atmosphere, some of which are known to have links with cancer in humans, such as dioxins released from certain plastics and electrical components. Modern incinerators are able to reduce such emissions, but they still produce a toxic ash which must then be disposed of by other means.

THINKING AHEAD

Incinerating or burying waste does not solve the current waste problem, but by contaminating the surrounding environments simply shifts it for future generations to deal with. For waste to be managed more sustainably it is important that those creating wastes today think ahead and search for alternatives that do not pass on the problems to future generations. The responsibility lies with today's generations (people like you and me) to consider our lifestyles, limit the amount of wastes we generate, and dispose of those we do create in a safe and sustainable manner.

weblinks

To learn more about MSW disposal go to www.epa.gov/epaoswer/non-hw/muncpl/index.htm

A waste circuit board from the United States or Europe releases toxic fumes as it is burned in Guangdong, China, to recover parts.

Toward sustainable waste

ENVIRONMENTALISTS HAVE BEEN CAMPAIGNING for more sustainable methods of waste management since the 1960s. It was at around this time that a number of high-profile cases of waste disasters began to persuade people that the way waste was handled must change.

A woman holds a victim of Minamata disease, which provided early global warnings about the problems of uncontrolled wastes.

WARNING SIGNS

One of the earliest waste disasters began in 1953 when residents living in the Japanese fishing village of Minamata began to complain of illnesses such as headaches, convulsions, and even blindness. By 1966, forty-three people had died and sixty-six had become permanently disabled by their illnesses. By 1983, the death toll had passed three hundred and as many as six thousand claimed to be suffering illnesses and disabilities. This terrible human tragedy was caused by a nearby chemical factory discharging waste methyl mercury into the waters around Minamata. The poisonous mercury was absorbed into the food chain and poisoned the local inhabitants when they ate fish captured in the area.

At a more global level, Scandinavia alerted the world to the problem of acid rain. This is caused by waste gases (mainly nitrogen oxides (NOx) and sulphur dioxide (SO_2) that are emitted when fossil fuels are burned). When these are released into the atmosphere they mix with water vapor to form an acidic solution that falls to the ground as rain, snow, or fog. In the 1950s, people across Scandinavia began to notice that fish in many lakes were disappearing. This was due to the lakes becoming too acidic as a result of acid rain. In Sweden today, some 14,000 lakes suffer from the effects of acidification and the same is true for many lakes across other countries in Scandinavia, as well as the United Kingdom and parts of North America.

What makes acid rain a particularly interesting example is that it is long-distance waste. The gases causing acid rain often affect areas far from their source as they are carried on the wind to distant locations. In Scandinavia, for example, it is estimated that 90 percent of acid rain is caused by waste emissions blown mainly from the United Kingdom, Germany, and Poland. The experience of acid rain in Scandinavia alerted the world to the fact that some wastes were a regional or even global problem and would require international cooperation to solve them.

── weblinks ──

To find out more about acid rain
go to www.ec.gc.ca/acidrain

DATABANK

A survey of European forests in 1999 revealed that one in four trees were damaged (suffering loss of leaves or needles). Acid rain was thought to be among the major causes.

These trees in the Harz mountains of Germany have been damaged by acid rain.

A roadside sign, part of a local campaign, protests the building of a new incinerator in County Tipperary, Ireland.

CALL TO ACTION

Waste issues are today among the biggest concerns of environmental organizations around the world. Greenpeace, for example, has had a long-standing campaign against the nuclear energy industry and the

wastes it generates. Friends of the Earth, meanwhile, highlights waste as one of its priority campaigns with particular attention to the problems of landfill and incineration of mixed waste. More recently a number of organizations have been established that focus solely on the problems of waste. In the United Kingdom, for example, Waste Watch was established in 1987 to promote greater awareness of waste reduction, reuse and recycling — the so-called three Rs. In the United States, a similar, internet-based organization called Zero Waste America (ZWA) was established in 1996.

As public awareness of waste issues has increased so too has their concern to do something about it. In particular, people have become concerned about the handling of waste in their own communities. Numerous local campaign groups have developed as a result. In fact, so widespread are such campaigns that there is probably one in your own community or a neighboring one. A problem with many such campaigns is that their concern is with waste handling facilities close to where they live rather than with the problems associated with waste overall. Many of those involved in such campaigns would not have considered waste issues had they not been so close to home. This way of thinking has been given a special name: NIMBY, meaning Not In My Back Yard.

SPEAKING UP

Proposals for new waste incinerators or landfill sites often spark NIMBY campaigns in surrounding communities. Some of these have been extremely successful, such as the Guildford Anti-Incinerator Network (GAIN) in the United Kingdom. The actions of GAIN and its supporters helped to prevent the construction of a waste incinerator in their neighborhood, but, more importantly, the attention given to waste issues has started a detailed debate on making the town of Guildford (near London) into a zero-waste community. The success of GAIN also inspired a local musician, Niamh Clune, to write a song called "We Are The Voice" to encourage others to speak out on environmental issues. The song was performed at the opening ceremony to the World Summit on Sustainable Development in Johannesburg, South Africa, in August 2002.

weblinks

For more information about the World Summit go to www.johannesburgsummit.org

OPINION

'GAIN and its thousands of supporters will never give up the fight to prevent our children being exposed to the dangers of incinerator pollution and to develop alternative solutions.'

Colin Matthews, Chairman of GAIN

Resistance to waste facilities in local neighborhoods such as here in New York have become known as NIMBY campaigns.

LOOKING TO ALTERNATIVES

While the public is often quick to oppose mixed waste handling facilities such as incinerators and landfills, the public response to alternatives is often less immediate. For example, many people know about the benefits of recycling, but fail to recycle everything that they could. Similarly, many people choose not to buy goods made with recycled materials as they believe they are of lower quality than goods made with raw materials. Such attitudes will have to change dramatically if waste is to be sustainably managed in the future.

Progress has already been made in encouraging people to consider the alternatives to waste disposal. The most obvious example of this is recycling and today, in more-developed countries at least, recycling bins are a common feature in many villages, towns, and cities. These provide central collection points for people to sort and recycle some of the main items found in a typical household's waste such as glass, paper, cans, and clothes.

Recycling of glass is practiced by many people, but in reality is only a very minor solution to the bigger waste problem.

Curbside recycling programs — where households sort waste into different materials for collection from outside their houses — have also become popular in some countries. In the United States, for example, the number of curbside collection programs grew from just 1,000 in 1988 to over 9,000 by 1998. The curbside programs have helped the United States achieve significant improvements in its recycling of MSW which increased from just 8 percent in 1990 to around 32 percent by 2001. Similar programs have helped other countries, including Switzerland, Holland, and Germany recycle over 50 percent of their MSW.

A GOOD START?

Recycling is certainly a good start in the struggle to solve the waste problem, but it is only a start. Recycling rates often only apply to MSW, which in turn makes up only a small proportion of the total waste generated within a country. In the United States, for example, the Environmental Protection Agency (EPA) has estimated that MSW makes up only around 2 percent of all U.S. waste. The other problem with recycling is that although it has increased in most countries, so too has the amount of waste being generated in the first place.

DATABANK

In Australia, around 60 percent of MSW is recycled following the introduction of curbside collection programs during the 1990s.

For example, in Norway between 1995 and 1998, the total amount of waste generated increased by three times more than the amount that was recycled over the same period.

A U.S. family with their typical weekly groceries. The packaged goods create a large amount of waste, including a growing amount of plastics.

BEYOND RECYCLING

Perhaps the greatest challenge to creating a future in which waste is sustainably managed is to move people beyond the relatively easy task of recycling. A far greater impact can be had by reducing the amount of waste produced in the first place and making the remaining waste easier to manage. Some waste reduction measures are very simple, such as refusing plastic bags when offered them in a shop or using public transport instead of private vehicles to reduce harmful emissions. Others are more complex, such as dealing with the excessive packaging that many products (especially supermarket foods) are sold in. To reduce wastes such as these, businesses and industries will have to become actively involved in trying to reduce the amount of waste their products create.

GROWING MOUNTAINS

Reducing the amount of waste produced is essential to stop the growing mountains of waste that today plague so many

Most of the waste generated by the week's food shopping for this Turkish family is biodegradable and so has relatively little environmental impact.

countries. The problem is most serious in the more developed countries where the amount of waste generated per person increased by around 22 percent between 1980 and 2000, and is set to increase by a further 30 percent by 2020. In some countries the problems due to not acting are already clear. In New York, for example, landfill sites are now full and so the city has started transporting its waste beyond the city limits. A convoy of delivery trucks, that if put together would stretch for almost 19 miles, carries away around 11,000 tons of waste every day to landfill sites up to 300 miles away. In the United Kingdom, too, numerous landfill sites will be full before 2010 if waste production continues at present levels.

FORCING CHANGE

Some of those most concerned about the waste problem suggest that after over thirty years of persuading people to reduce wastes it is time for governments to take more direct actions that will force changes. They argue that by taxing any wasteful and polluting activities governments are able to influence businesses, industries and individuals alike to change their attitudes toward waste. Such direct actions are gaining in popularity and demonstrate a willingness to take the waste problem more seriously.

Sustainable waste in practice

F<small>EW PEOPLE WOULD DISAGREE</small> with the need to reduce waste, but turning this into practice is more complicated because many people are used to lifestyles that generate a great deal of waste. The challenge is to persuade people to adopt lower-waste lifestyles, but some resist such changes in the belief that it would mean a lower quality of life. In fact, evidence suggests this is far from true and that a low-waste lifestyle normally improves quality of life as it creates a cleaner and healthier society and saves money for both individuals and governments.

WASTE NOT, WANT NOT

People in less developed countries produce, on the whole, far less waste than those living in more developed countries. This is partly because they are less wealthy and so their consumption levels are considerably lower. However, it is also because they value resources more highly and often do not treat them as wastes at all. Across much of Africa, for example, containers such as the plastic drums that

A water seller in Kano, Nigeria, reuses plastic drums that once contained vegetable oil to transport water to his customers.

food oil comes in are cleaned out and sold as strong and durable water containers. Old tires are used to make tough rubber sandals, and the tires' reinforcing wires are stripped out and used to make fishing baskets. Tin cans are reused to make small oil lamps while bigger pieces of metal are beaten into shape to make small stoves. In fact, almost anything that can be used again will be — this philosophy helps to keep waste levels relatively low. In creating a more sustainable future there is much that could be learned from people who have for many years, found creative ways of reusing resources instead of just dumping them as wastes.

THE THREE Rs

The most frequently used model for a sustainable waste policy is that of the three Rs: reduce, reuse, recycle. This simple order of priority says we should first try to reduce the amount of waste produced, second, look for ways to reuse wastes, and third, recycle as much waste as possible. Only then should any remaining products be disposed of as genuine waste, but even these can have uses as we shall see. Let us now look at each of the three Rs in more detail.

Buying unpackaged fruit and vegetables reduces household waste and is often cheaper, too.

WASTE REDUCTION

The most efficient way to tackle waste is to reduce the amount produced in the first place. Most industries, businesses, and households could significantly reduce the wastes they produce with relatively minor changes in the way they operate. Where this has been done, substantial financial savings have often been made. Households, for example, can purchase frequently used goods such as toilet paper, cleaning products, and basic foods (cereals, milk, pasta, etc.) in bulk. This reduces the amount of packaging waste and will often prove cheaper, too. They can also look for products that have less packaging waste, such as fresh fruit and vegetables, instead of packaged ones.

For businesses, reducing wastes not only benefits the environment but makes good business sense, too. This is because waste disposal is an expensive process, especially when toxic or hazardous materials require special treatment. A good example of this is the U.S.-based 3M corporation which makes a variety of goods from stationery supplies to health products. In 1975, they began a 3P program — Pollution Prevention Pays — in their factories that by the early 1990s had reduced pollutants by over 600,000 tons and saved around $500 million. They further reduced waste in the 1990s and continue to set ambitious waste reduction targets into the future.

Industries are now beginning to cooperate on waste reduction, too. In Germany, for example, water companies serving Munich, Leipzig, and Osnabrück are now paying local farmers to practice organic farming. This is because organic farming does not use harmful chemicals, many of which are absorbed into local water supplies as wastes. It is cheaper for the water companies to work with farmers to encourage waste reduction than it is to clean farm chemicals out of the water supply.

Xerox, a major world supplier of office machinery, introduced tough waste reduction policies in 1991 and extended these to its suppliers in 1998. These included reductions in packaging, the elimination of toxic wastes, and the clear marking of recyclable plastics used in their products. By 2000, these policies had helped Xerox to achieve recycling rates of 80 percent for its solid waste and to reduce air emissions by 89 percent between 1991 and 2001.

These washable diapers are a sustainable alternative to disposable diapers which can take up to five hundred years to decompose in a land-fill site. In the United Kingdom, some 8 million disposable diapers are thrown away every day.

DATABANK

As a result of its waste reduction policies, Xerox was able to generate cost savings of approximately $47 million in 1999.

DATABANK

An average fleece jacket may contain the reused material from around twenty-five plastic drink bottles.

and reused as the raw material for manufacturing popular fleece clothing.

FOLLOWING NATURE

In nature, wastes are continually reused or recycled within local and global ecosystems: the wastes from one part of the ecosystem becomes a resource for another. As concern about sustainability has increased, businesses and industries are now looking closely at how they can follow the good example set by natural systems. They are realizing that it is better to think of waste as a resource and to find new or alternative uses for it rather than disposing of it. In the textile industry, for example, plastic (Polyethylene Terephthalate, or PET for short) drink bottles are melted down

SETTING AN EXAMPLE

The idea of copying nature is perhaps best represented by the Danish industrial town of Kalundborg. Beginning in the 1970s, the town developed one of the best-known waste reuse systems in the world — a system still in use today. At the center of the system is the Asnæs coal-fired power station (the largest in Denmark) and the neighboring Statoil oil refinery. Owing to a shortage of water in the region, Statoil supplies its treated wastewater to Asnæs for use in its cooling process. In return, Asnæs supplies Statoil with waste steam for use in its refining process. The waste steam is also supplied to a nearby chemical company and to around 20,000 households in Kalundborg itself where it forms part of a district heating system.

The reuse does not stop there however. The waste gases from the Statoil refinery are used as a cleaner fuel for the Asnæs power station and by Gyproc, whose nearby factory makes plasterboard for the building industry. Gyproc also purchases one of their raw materials (calcium sulphate or gypsum) from Asnæs who produces it as a waste from a process called desulphurization (removal of sulphur from coal that is released during its burning). Other partners in the Kalundborg system include a local fish farm, some commercial greenhouses, a chemicals company, and a pharmaceutical plant. It has been estimated that by 1995, around 3 million tons of waste were transferred for reuse every year. Kalundborg stands as a good example of how wastes need not be a problem, but can in fact benefit others through their reuse as a valuable economic resource.

---

weblinks

To find out more about waste reuse go to
www.wasteguide.org.uk

The Asnæs power station and Statoil refinery are at the heart of Kalundborg, Denmark's resource, reuse network.

A store owner in Nigeria shows off his shoes. He imports shoes that have been thrown away from Europe, and reconditions them to be sold and used again.

EXTENDED LIFE

Another form of reuse is to give products an extended life. For example, the office machinery company Xerox now takes back all of their old machines. They are taken apart for use as spares or are repaired and cleaned for sale as remanufactured mach-ines. Xerox's new machines are designed to be reused in this way and so reduce wastes and provide less expensive business machines for those who cannot afford new ones. A similar program called Fonebak was launched in the United Kingdom in September 2002 to reuse discarded cell phones by reconditioning them and sending them for resale in less-developed countries.

The life of a product can also be extended by repairing it instead of disposing of it. Many goods could be easily and cheaply repaired and continue to provide a useful service for many years. Many companies now offer extended warranties to encourage the repair of their goods. Repairing goods also provides valuable jobs and reduces the use of raw materials needed to make replacement goods.

Offering used goods to charities is another way to ensure that goods have an extended life and also benefit people in your own community or around the world.

NEW LIFE

If waste products or materials cannot be reused, the next best thing is to look for ways to give them new life by recycling them. The ability to recycle depends on two main factors: the material in question and the market for recycled materials. Some materials such as glass, metals, and paper are relatively easy to recycle and there is a reasonably good demand for them. Aluminum, for example, used in soft drink cans among other things, can be endlessly recycled and made into new aluminum products. Using recycled aluminum also saves on energy, using up to 95 percent less than is needed to make the same product with raw materials. Glass, too, can be repeatedly recycled, though in most circumstances it must first be sorted into different color types. Paper, one of the most commonly recycled products, can only be recycled about four times before it begins to break down and deteriorate in quality, but this still helps to safeguard forests for future use.

DATABANK

Enough aluminum is thrown away by Americans every three months to rebuild the entire United States commercial airline fleet.

This gold was reclaimed from cell phones that were discarded in Japan. Silver and other precious metals are also collected for reuse.

29

These tires will be burned to provide energy, but more innovative and less polluting uses are now being developed.

INNOVATIONS IN RECYCLING

Materials such as plastics are much harder to recycle. This is partly because there are many different types and they cannot be mixed. Plastics are also often only part of a product, such as the casing for a computer or cell phone, which means they need separating before they can be recycled. As the recycling industry grows it is creating innovative new methods and uses for the recycling of more difficult wastes. For example, HDPE (High Density Polyethylene) plastics such as those used for shampoo and milk bottles can now be recycled into a strong and durable material known as plastic lumber. This is increasingly used for things such as picnic benches, decking, small foot and bicycle bridges, fencing, and signs.

Another waste product that has seen considerable progress in recycling is tires. In Western Europe alone an estimated 200 million tires are disposed of each year with close to 60 percent of them ending up in landfill sites or being burned to generate energy. By breaking down tires and producing a substance called rubber crumb, however, it is possible to recycle them for a wide range of uses. For example, they are used to make shock-absorbent surfaces for playgrounds and sports facilities or for the rubber backing of carpets and floor tiles. And new uses are being found all the time, such as in the United States where rubber crumb is mixed with asphalt to make a tough and durable road surface. In 2001, around 10 million tires a year were being used in this process.

BACK TO BASICS

Recycling is not just about new technologies, however. One of the most basic forms of recycling is composting, the natural breakdown of organic material such as fruit, vegetable, and garden wastes into nutrient rich soil. In the United Kingdom, around 38 percent of domestic waste is thought to be organic content suitable for composting and yet in 1999 less than 3 percent of domestic waste was composted in municipal or community programs.

This figure does not include households who compost their own waste in a compost bin, but there is still great scope to increase composting levels. Compost bins are a particularly good way to compost kitchen waste, such as vegetable peelings, as they take up little room, are very efficient and can even be used indoors by people who do not have a garden.

---
weblinks

For more information on composting go to
www.epa.gov/epaoswer/non-hw/compost

Kitchen waste disposed of in compost bins emerges as compost and liquid fertilizer at the bottom in as little as ten weeks.

Making sustainable waste work

THERE IS GREAT PROMISE FOR IMPROVING recycling technology and methods in the future, but of equal, if not greater importance, is the challenge to change people's behavior and attitude toward waste. If people begin demanding solutions to waste problems then it will encourage governments, industries, and businesses to develop such solutions.

MIXED MESSAGES

Evidence suggests that people would like to manage their waste more sustainably. In England and Wales, a survey by the Environment Agency found that nine out of ten people would recycle more if it were made easier. Despite this positive support, however, the United Kingdom has a poor

A local authority recycling center in Weymouth, United Kingdom, collects many products that would otherwise be thrown away.

A coal-fired power station in Queensland, Australia. Australia has yet to agree to the Kyoto Protocol for reducing CO_2 emissions.

record on waste, with a recycling rate of only 11 percent and a waste mountain that is set to grow by around 1 million tons a year. Other countries suffer similar contradictions between the attitudes and actions of their public. With such mixed messages on waste there is clearly a need for some form of intervention to encourage or even force more sustainable waste management.

TARGETING WASTE

One relatively simple form of intervention is the setting of waste targets. In the United Kingdom, the government has set a target to recycle 25 percent of household waste by 2005, putting pressure on all households, businesses, and local authorities to do much better than at present. As awareness of waste issues grows, most countries have now adopted waste targets of one form or another and some have even been adopted at a larger level. In the European Union (EU), for example, there are targets for the reduction and recycling of packaging waste and for the reuse and recycling of electrical wastes and even motor vehicles when they reach the end of their useful life.

At a broader level, international targets have been agreed to reduce some of the problems associated with waste. The Kyoto Protocol, for example, has set a target for reducing emissions of carbon dioxide to 5 percent below their 1990 levels by 2008–12. Although several nations have yet to agree to the Kyoto Protocol (most notably the United States, Australia, and Russia) it still marks an important international commitment to reducing wastes.

GETTING TOUGH

Targets can be useful in highlighting areas where waste management needs to be improved, but as with many targets they are not always met and can be difficult to enforce. Some environmentalists believe

A man uses a swipe card to deposit waste in a community underground dumpster in Weert, The Netherlands.

that in order for real changes to be made, governments must get tough on waste and not rely on the voluntary actions of businesses and individuals. Where this has been done, substantial benefits have been seen. In Switzerland fines of around 100 Swiss francs ($55) are imposed on households if they do not properly separate their waste for recycling and disposal. In Einzkries, Germany, household garbage cans are fitted with an electronic system that measures the volume of waste disposed of and charges the residents accordingly. A similar program based on underground community dumpsters in the Netherlands has been growing in popularity since it was started in 1997. Residents access the underground dumpsters by swiping an electronic card to open them. The dumpster calculates the amount of waste that is deposited and coverts it into a charge to be paid by the household. In 1998 there were around 4,000 such bins in operation, but by September 2001 this had increased to 24,500 dumpsters, reaching around 8 percent of the Dutch population.

POLLUTER PAYS PRINCIPLE

The idea behind the policies used in the examples above is known as the polluter pays principle (PPP). This simply means that those who produce the most pollution (waste in this instance) should pay for it accordingly. It also means that individuals, businesses, and industries that make efforts to reduce their waste output will end up paying less for waste disposal. PPP systems are therefore seen as encouraging greater uptake of the three Rs (see page 23). The benefits of policies based on PPP can be felt relatively quickly.

In Ireland, for example, a 0.15 (approximately $.16) Euro tax on plastic shopping bags introduced in March 2002, had, by the end of 2002, led to a tenfold reduction in the number of plastic bags used by Irish shoppers. On a broader scale the impact of applying the polluter pays principle to waste policy can clearly be seen in those countries where it has been tried. It is no coincidence that Switzerland, Germany, and The Netherlands (the three examples given earlier) have some of the highest recycling rates in the world.

> **OPINION**
>
> The reduction [in plastic bags] has been immediate and the positive visual impact on the environment is plain to see. We are realizing that by implementing practical measures such as this, the environment wins.
>
> Martin Cullen, Irish Environment Minister

A customer in Ireland shows a strong reusable bag used for grocery shopping. The use of such bags has increased following a tax on disposable bags introduced in 2002.

can prove unpopular, however, and Denmark has been in a long legal battle with the European Union which says the can ban is unfair on companies that produce their products in cans and wish to sell them in Denmark. In 2002, the Danish government was finally forced to abolish the can ban. Interested in continuing their waste reduction policies, however, a refundable tax has been imposed on all cans to encourage people to return them for recycling. The government hopes that this deposit-and-return system will lead to 95 percent of drink cans being returned to stores for recycling.

TAX SHIFTING

Some governments are concerned that introducing tough new policies on waste may prove unpopular with consumers (who are also the voters who keep them in power). This is especially true if the policies involve charging people more for the wastes they produce. One way to overcome this problem is tax shifting. This is where governments raise taxes on environmentally damaging practices (such as waste generation) and in return lower taxes on incomes or products and services that benefit the environment. Tax shifting,

BANNING WASTE

Some governments have made the decision to ban certain types of waste altogether by imposing laws on how products are sold. In Denmark, the government imposed a ban on drink cans in 1977 in favor of reusable bottles that reduce the amount of waste generated and so have less environmental impact. Such decisions

DATABANK

By 2002, Germany had shifted 2 percent of its taxes onto environmentally destructive activities and as a result managed to reduce taxes on people's incomes by the same amount.

like PPP, can have a rapid impact on consumer behavior.

In the United Kingdom a lower tax on ultra low sulphur diesel (ULSD) than on normal diesel led to a rapid increase in ULSD sales from 5 percent of diesel sales in July 1998 to 43 percent by February 1999. By 2000, the whole of the United Kingdom had converted to ULSD and so reduced sulphur emissions (one of the main waste gases responsible for acid rain) considerably. By applying tax shifting to energy use as a whole, several countries including Norway, Sweden, Germany, Italy, and Finland have managed substantial reductions in their emissions of waste gases. For example, Finland introduced the first ever tax on CO_2 in 1990, and as a result had cut emissions by 7 percent by 1998.

Cleaner diesel is now used by all diesel vehicles in the United Kingdom. A government tax on dirtier diesel helped to influence this change.

OPINION

It is increasingly clear...that countries are recognizing the power of tax systems...for shaping [the] economic decisions of individuals and businesses.

Bernie Fischlowitz-Roberts,
Earth Policy Institute, United States

This woman finds a label that tells her the envelopes she is looking to buy are made with recycled paper.

KNOWLEDGE FOR ACTION

A major barrier to waste reduction is that people often lack the knowledge of how to go about it. There is a need to fill this information gap if sustainable waste management is to become a reality in the early twenty-first century. In truth, many opportunities and facilities for waste reduction exist on people's own doorsteps — they are just not aware of them. Governments, local authorities and those directly involved in waste management are now working to overcome such problems. In the United Kingdom a service for people to find recycling facilities using the Internet was launched in 2000 by a partnership of waste organizations, local authorities, and over 700 businesses. Visitors to recycling websites simply type in their postal code and the products they wish to recycle, and the service provides details of the nearest appropriate facility.

Most local authorities now provide information about waste reduction programs and recycling facilities to residents living in their area. Many operate their own curbside or communal programs or have information about private programs operating in their area. Many are also involved in direct education projects such as schools programs to teach young people about the benefits of the three Rs. You may have experienced such a program in your own school or community.

weblinks

To find out more about recycling go to www.grrn.org/kids_recycle/index.htm

The office supplier, Staples, is one of many businesses that today use and offer an increasing number of recycled products.

CLOSING THE LOOP

One important area in which information needs to be improved is in raising awareness of where to buy products made from recycled materials. Recycling will only work properly when there is greater demand for the products made from recycled materials. This need is often referred to as closing the loop, so that people not only recycle, but purchase goods made from recyclable materials too. Numerous directories (many of them on the Internet) now exist to help consumers find and buy recycled produce. These are often aimed at households, but an increasing number are encouraging businesses and industries to buy recycled, too. Some companies have adopted their own policies to promote recycled goods such as Staples, an office supply company — one of the biggest in the world with over 1,400 stores in six countries. In 2002, around 1,000 of the 7,500 products that Staples stocked were recycled or contained recycled materials. The company also sponsors America Recycles Day, a day to raise awareness of recycling and recycled products.

weblinks

To find out more about America Recycles Day go to www.americarecyclesday.org

Sustainable waste and you

Consumers like you and me have an important role to play in the future of waste management. We are able to send signals that will influence the actions of businesses, industries, and governments alike to do something about waste issues. We are also able to take more direct actions ourselves.

This German supermarket encourages recycling of excess packaging before shoppers even leave the store. Such programs can help make recycling part of peoples' everyday routines.

CONSUMER POWER

Consumers are an extremely powerful force because their buying decisions can persuade manufacturers and retailers to change the ways in which they operate. After all, without contented customers, businesses would very quickly begin to lose money and may even go out of business. Many consumers do not realize the power they have to influence change for the better and so businesses often continue wasteful practices such as the use of excessive packaging.

ACTIONS SPEAK LOUDLY

Our actions are of great importance and it is arguably here that consumers have the greatest power. For example,

Refusing disposable bags and using your own reusable bags instead is a positive way to cut down on waste.

by purchasing goods that have less packaging, consumers send clear signals to manufacturers and retailers that they do not want the waste associated with heavily packaged goods. In the United Kingdom, a survey conducted in 2002 indicated that almost 90 percent of consumers thought it was important that the supermarket where they regularly shopped was concerned about its effect on the environment.

With such high expectations, many supermarkets have begun to adopt various policies that promote the three Rs. Most now have reusable bag-for-life programs whereby customers buy stronger plastic bags and reuse them until they break. The supermarket will then replace the bag free of charge when it is returned for recycling.

Recycling facilities are also a common sight at most supermarkets today and many offer in-store recycling facilities for their disposable plastic bags. One British chain, the Co-op, is particularly dedicated to promote the three Rs. In addition to promoting the use of recycled product packaging where possible, in 2002 it introduced the United Kingdom's first degradable plastic bag which takes just three years to degrade and leaves no toxins in the environment. This compares with over a hundred years before a normal disposable shopping bag even begins to break down.

LOCAL ACTION

Doing your part

There are many ways that you can reduce wastes, but here are a few ideas to help get you started.

- Look for products that have less packaging, such as fruits and vegetables.

- Buy in bulk products your family regularly uses to reduce packaging waste.

- Think before you buy! Do you really need it or could you rent or borrow an item instead?

- Have goods repaired rather than throwing them away and buy better made and more durable goods that have a longer lifespan.

- Ask retailers about their waste policies and whether their products are recyclable.

- Find out about recycled goods and buy them where possible.

- Join your local recycling service or take recycled waste to your nearest recycling center.

- Set up a garden compost bin to recycle organic kitchen waste.

A display in Copenhagen, Denmark, is used to demonstrate how much litter is left in public places every day.

WORDS COUNT

On top of our actions, words are also very important. For example, when you go shopping you can refuse to accept a carrier bag for your goods and instead bring your own, or consider whether you even need one for smaller items that may fit in your pocket instead. Words can also be important in influencing waste policies in your own community. If you are concerned about the levels of waste or the lack of recycling facilities, for example, write to your local authority to find out what is being done about the situation, or even make some suggestions yourself.

You could have a similar influence in your school by suggesting that they conduct a survey of their waste patterns and look for ways to improve on them. The school could even earn money from recycling or setting up its own community recycling program. In the U.K. county of Suffolk, for example, Elmsett School, with just sixty pupils, has established a very successful school recycling center. The center serves the local community and is supported by the local authority and nearby businesses. Money raised from the sale of the recycled goods has been used to purchase new school equipment, to fund a part-time teacher, and is now being saved to help fund a new school building.

---
weblinks

To find out more about school recycling go to www.ofee.gov/whats/newschoolrecycle.htm

---

A stall at a Green Gathering in Wiltshire, United Kingdom, sells clothing made from recycled fabrics that would otherwise be treated as waste.

Sustainable waste and the future

W E HAVE SEEN IN THIS BOOK that waste is a major challenge for this century and one that cannot be ignored. The world is already overflowing with waste, and much of it will still be around in hundreds or even thousands of years. This is far from sustainable and is polluting the land, water, and air that all human and animal life depends on for their survival.

A GROWING PROBLEM

The problem with waste is that it is being generated at a rate faster than solutions to waste problems are being found. Some places such as Hong Kong, The Netherlands, and parts of the United States and the United Kingdom, are literally running out of room to dispose of waste. There is no doubt that recycling has increased dramatically over the last thirty years and continues to do so, but if more waste is being produced at the same time, then the impact is only minimal. The key to a sustainable future is to reduce the amount of waste being produced in the first place and this will demand major changes in consumption pat-

Litter on a beach along Venezuela's Caribbean coast is a reminder of the worldwide waste problem.

A market booth in Greenwich, London, sells toys, ornaments, and even handbags, all made from colorful recycled tins and soft-drink cans.

terns and attitudes toward waste. Countries such as Switzerland, The Netherlands, and Germany have demonstrated that such changes can take place, and over a relatively short time, too. The key to their success has a great deal to do with the commitment shown by their governments, but it also relies on the cooperation of citizens like you and me.

SUSTAINABLE SOLUTIONS

Business and industries are slowly finding sustainable solutions to the problems of waste, such as the development of plastic lumber, degradable plastic bags, and road surfaces made from old tires. Financial incentives such as taxes and grants can be used to accelerate this process and are now being used in many countries as they struggle to meet national or international targets for waste reduction such as the Kyoto Protocol. The public, too, is involved in finding new uses for wastes including some creative solutions where wastes are being turned into toys or even art works. Perhaps the biggest change and the best solution to the waste problem is to stop thinking of goods as wastes. Instead we should think of them as resources that are simply waiting to be reused in one way or another. In this way, waste can make a valuable contribution to a more sustainable world.

Glossary

Acid rain Produced when pollutants such as sulphur dioxide and nitrogen oxides (emitted when fuels are burned) mix with water vapor in the air to form an acidic solution. It is damaging to plants, trees, lakes, and buildings.

Campaign A planned, organized action which aims to raise people's awareness of an issue.

Climate change The process of long-term changes to the world's climate (warming or cooling, etc.). Occurs naturally, but is today more as a result of human activities polluting the atmosphere.

Community A group of people who either live in the same area (e.g. village, town, or district), share common interests and beliefs (e.g. the importance of recycling waste) or share both these characteristics.

Compost A mixture of organic household waste (e.g. vegetable waste and brown cardboard) and plants that have decomposed over time.

Compost bin A sealed container in which organic kitchen waste is broken down into fertilizer.

Consumers People who buy or use a resource, product, or service.

Consumption The use of resources, products, and services by consumers.

Ecosystem The contents of an environment, including all the plants and animals that live there. This could be a garden pond, a forest, or Earth.

Emissions Polluting waste products (gas and solids) released into the environment. These include car exhaust and airplane fumes into the air and waste water and sewage into streams or the sea.

Food chain A series of organisms (plants and animals) each dependent on the next as a source of food.

Fossil fuels Fuels from the fossilized remains of plants and animals formed over millions of years. They include coal, oil, and natural gas. Once used they are gone: non-renewable.

Greenhouse gas An atmospheric gas that traps some of the heat radiating from the Earth's surface. Human activity has increased the level of greenhouses gases, such as carbon dioxide and methane, in the atmosphere

Hazardous Something that is dangerous to human health and/or the environment.

High Density Polyethylene (HDPE) A type of plastic used to make items such as bottles for shampoo, cosmetics, and milk.

Incinerator A furnace where waste is burnt at high temperatures.

Industrial Revolution The period in the late eighteenth century and early nineteenth century when new machinery and the use of fossil fuels to generate energy led to the start of modern industry and dramatic changes in the way people lived.

Kyoto Protocol Arising from a meeting held in Kyoto, Japan, in 1997. One hundred and sixty countries committed to reducing emissions of the six main greenhouse gases by 5.2 percent by 2012.

Landfill sites Holes in the ground used for burying waste. Once full they are covered over and the land is often used for building or leisure activities.

For further exploration

Leachate A liquid formed as rainwater passes through a landfill site and carries diluted chemicals and metals with it.

Municipal Solid Waste (MSW) The solid waste produced by homes, schools, offices, and shops.

Organic A product of living organisms that occurs naturally in the environment. Organic substances can be broken down by nature.

Packaging The container or wrapping that surrounds bought goods.

Polyethylene Terephthalate (PET) A type of plastic used to make soft drink bottles.

Radioactive substances Substances such as uranium or plutonium that emit energy in streams of radioactive particles. These particles are extremely harmful to humans and animals if they come into direct contact with them.

Recycling The collection and processing of used materials (e.g. glass, paper, cardboard and aluminium) so that they can be used again.

Resources The materials and energy used in making products or providing services.

Reuse To use something again, for the same or different purpose, instead of throwing it away.

Tailings The waste material from mining once the useful mineral has been extracted.

Toxin A poisonous substance which causes harm to human health and/or the environment.

White goods Domestic appliances such as washing machines, fridges, and freezers that are today found in most homes in developed countries.

Zero waste The recycling of all materials back into nature or the marketplace in a manner that protects human health and the environment.

Books to Read

Rob Bowden. *21st Century Debates: Waste, Recycling and Re-use.* London: Hodder Wayland, 2001.

Sally Morgan. *Earth Watch: Waste Disposal.* London: Franklin Watts, 2002.

Steve Parker. *Protecting Our Planet: Waste, Recycling and Re-use.* London: Hodder Wayland, 2001.

Index

The numbers in **bold** refer to photographs as well as text.